Dear Graduate: Life Lessons for a Happy Future

Be a Good Human Co
Books for thoughtful and socially-conscious kids.
BeAGoodHuman.Co

Text copyright © 2022 by Stacy Tornio

All rights reserved. No part of this book may be used or reproduced or transmitted in any form or by any means, electronic or mechanical, including photocopying and recording, without written consent from Be a Good Human Co.

Printed in the United States of America.

ISBN 978-1-7366934-6-9

THIS BOOK IS DEDICATED TO

_____

_____

_____

i WROTE THIS BOOK FOR JACK. i CAN'T WAIT TO SEE WHERE LIFE TAKES YOU.

LOVE, MOM

DEAR GRADUATE:

SOME OF LiFE'S BEST LESSONS ARE LEARNED OUTSiDE OF A CLASSROOM.

HERE ARE A FEW THAT MiGHT COME iN HANDY iN THE FUTURE.

GET UP FOR THE **SUNRISE.**

STAY OUT FOR THE **SUNSET.**

RESPECT OTHER CULTURES.

REMEMBER WHERE YOU CAME FROM, BUT DON'T LET IT GET IN THE WAY

OF WHERE YOU WANT TO GO.

PET A LOT OF DOGS.

Stacy wrote this book for her son, Jack, during his senior year of high school.

Learn more at BeAGoodHuman.co.

Made in the USA
Las Vegas, NV
05 May 2023